The ABC Hawai'i COLORING and Activity Book

illustrated by
Ruth Moen

Copyright © 2015 by BeachHouse Publishing
Illustrations © 2015 by Ruth Moen
No part of this book may be reproduced in any form
or by any electronic or mechanical means, including
information storage and retrieval devices or systems,
without prior written permission from the publisher,
except that brief passages may be quoted for reviews.

All rights reserved.

ISBN-10: 1-933067-66-7
ISBN-13: 978-1-933067-66-7

Fourth Printing, April 2018

BeachHouse Publishing, LLC
PO Box 5464
Kāne'ohe, Hawai'i 96744
Email: info@beachhousepublishing.com
www.beachhousepublishing.com

Printed by RRD Shenzhen, China

A is for Aloha

B is for Beach

Color by Numbers

1 = Red   2 = Blue   3 = Green   4 = Yellow   5 = Orange

C is for Canoe

1

One Angelfish

2

Two Butterflies

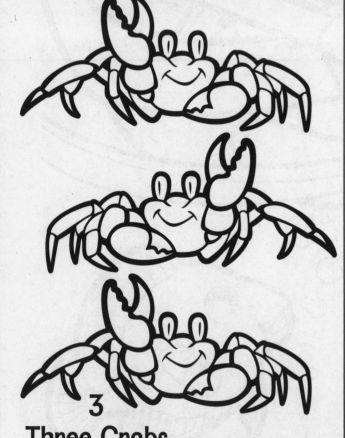

3

Three Crabs

4

Four Dolphins

Help this girl find her way to the sand castle.

Connect the Dots

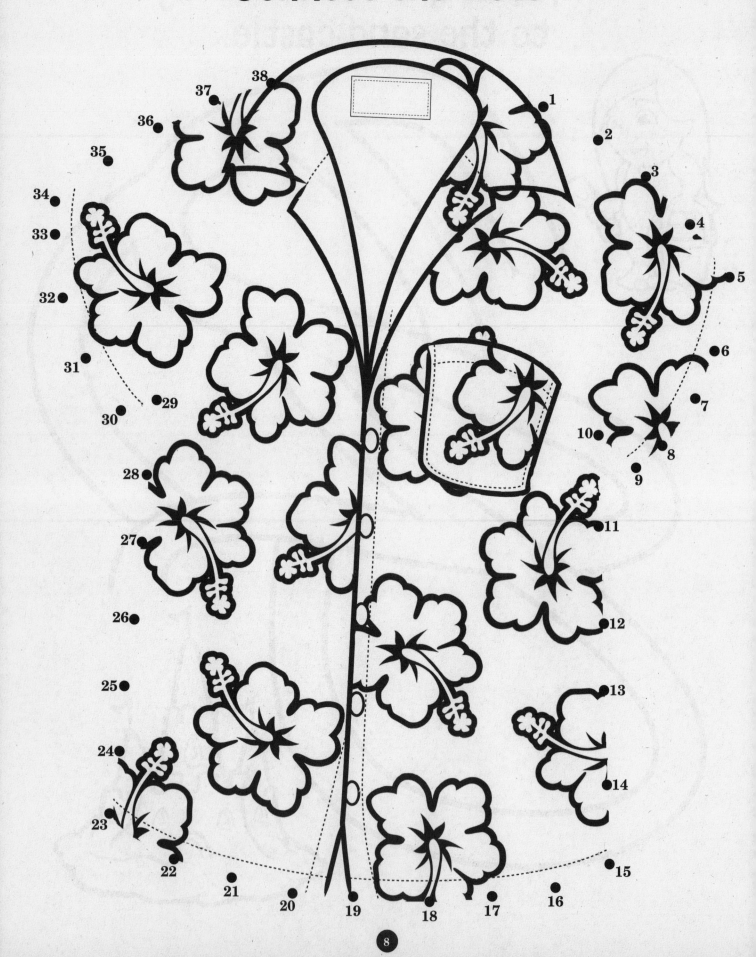

5

Five Anthurium

6

Six Bananas

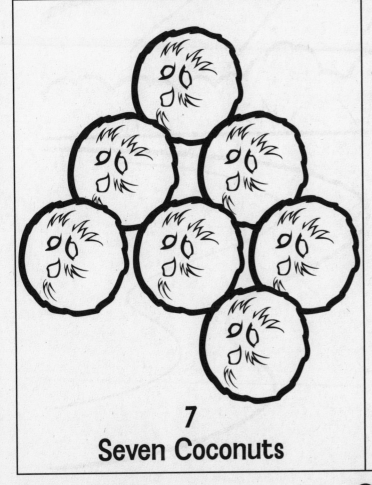

7

Seven Coconuts

8

Eight Dragonflies

D is for Diamond Head

E is for Egg

Match the person to the item.

Color by Numbers

1 = Yellow
2 = Red
3 = Blue
4 = Orange
5 = Purple

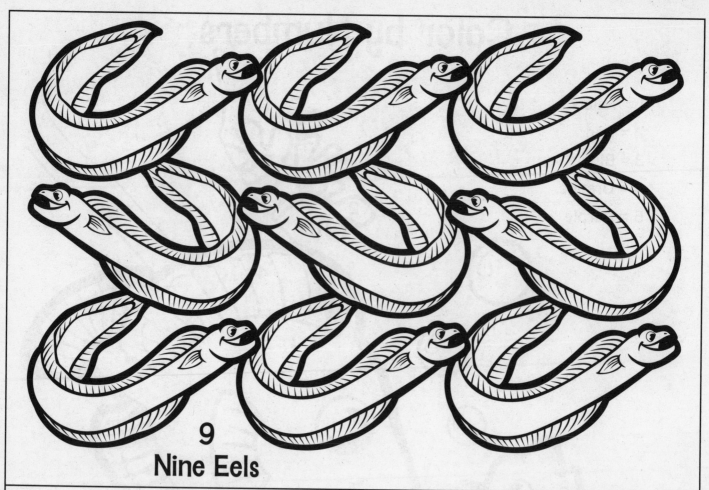

9
Nine Eels

10
Ten Flowers

F is for Fish

Which drawing is different?

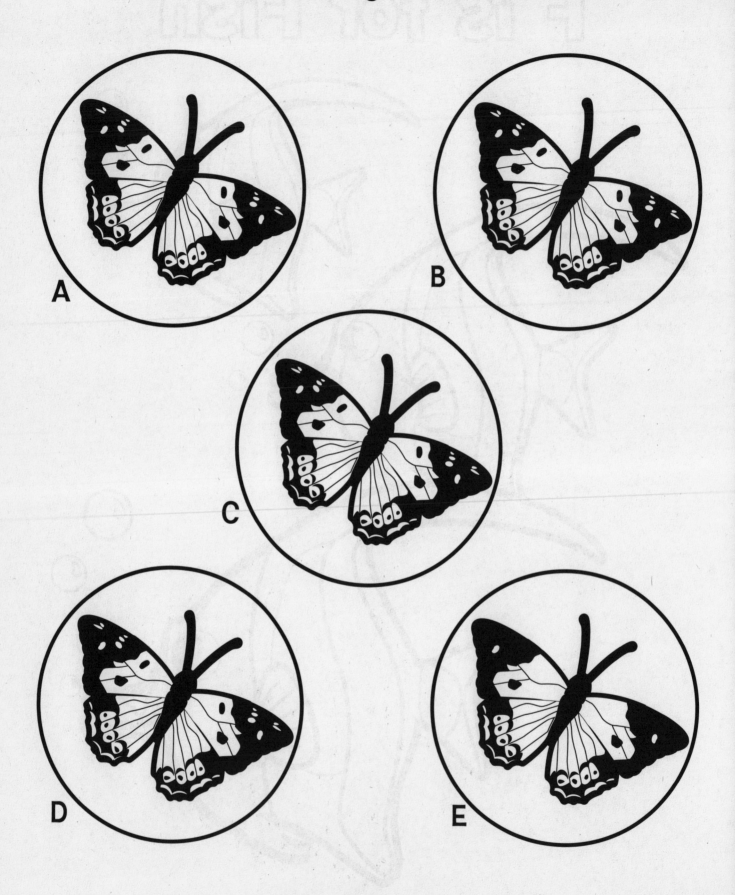

Solve the picture code to find out what type of fish a humuhumunukunukuāpuaʻa is.

I E R G T S H F

G is for Gecko

H is for Hula

1
One Goat

2
Two Honu (sea turtles)

3
Three Ipu

4
Four Jars of Jam

I is for Island

Connect the Dots

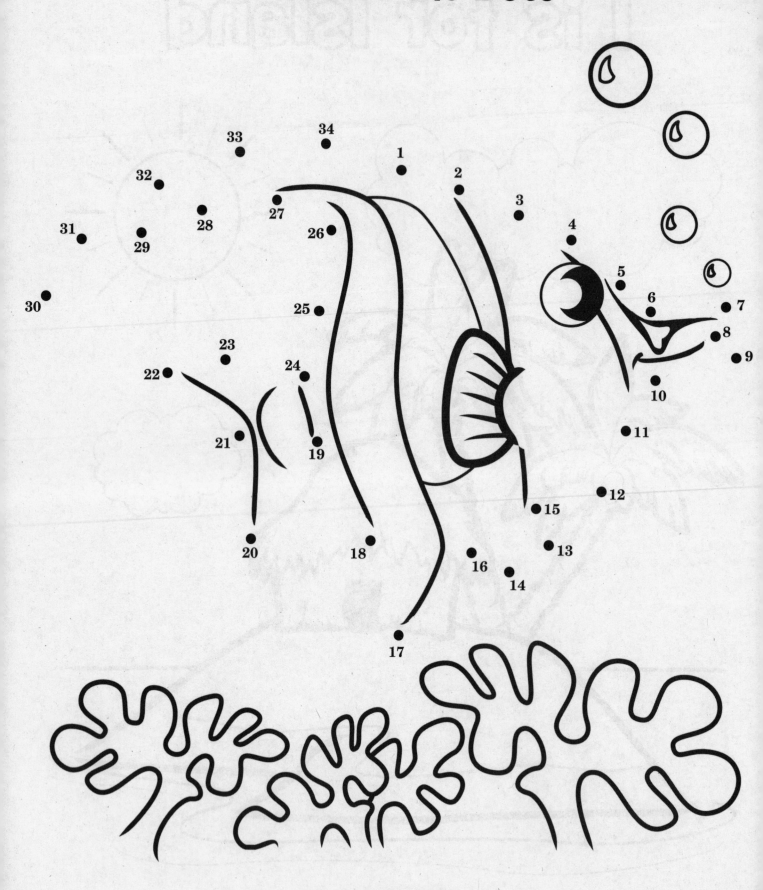

Time for some shave ice!
Find all 7 flavors.

```
C H E R R Y D F
O R Z Y B Q W O
C J G R A P E P
O V M A N G O A
N R X T A L Z P
U I S B N A W A
T Y G U A N I Y
C L I M E Y R A
```

 GRAPE   MANGO

 BANANA   PAPAYA

COCONUT   LIME

CHERRY

Answer

J is for Jellyfish

5
Five Keiki
(children)

6
Six Laulau

K is for Kitesurfing

Circle the 5 differences between these two pictures.

L is for Lei

7

Seven Mangoes

8

Eight Nēnē

M is for Mynah

Draw a line between each picture and its three close ups.

N is for Nai'a
(dolphin)

Color By Numbers

1 = Green   2 = Brown   3 = Yellow

33

O is for Octopus

9

Nine Owls

10

Ten Plumeria

Which path should the farmer take to pick the biggest pineapple?

P is for Peacock

Q is for Quilt

Connect the Dots

R is for Rainbow

1

One Queen

2

Two Rabbits

3

Three Sharks

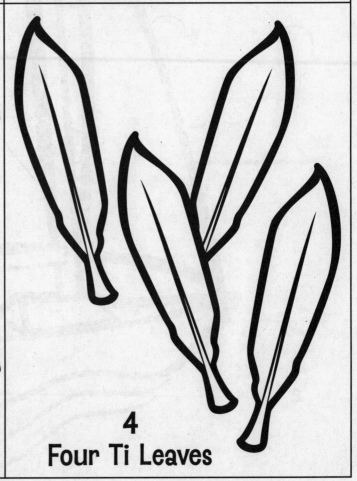

4

Four Ti Leaves

Color by Numbers

1 = Green   2 = Blue   3 = Red   4 = Yellow

Solve the picture code to learn the name of this surfing move.

O   E   S   H   T   N

_____

_____

S is for Surfboard

T is for Tiki

Draw lines from each picture to its three close-ups.

5
Five 'Ukulele

6
Six Vegetables

U is for 'Ukulele

Which image is different?

V is for Volcano

7

Seven Whales

Help these hikers find the waterfall.

W is for Waterfall

8
Eight X-rays

X is for Xylophone

9
Nine Yaks

Y is for Yellow Tang

Circle the 6 differences between these two pictures.

Z is for Zoo

Which path should these keiki take to see the elephant?

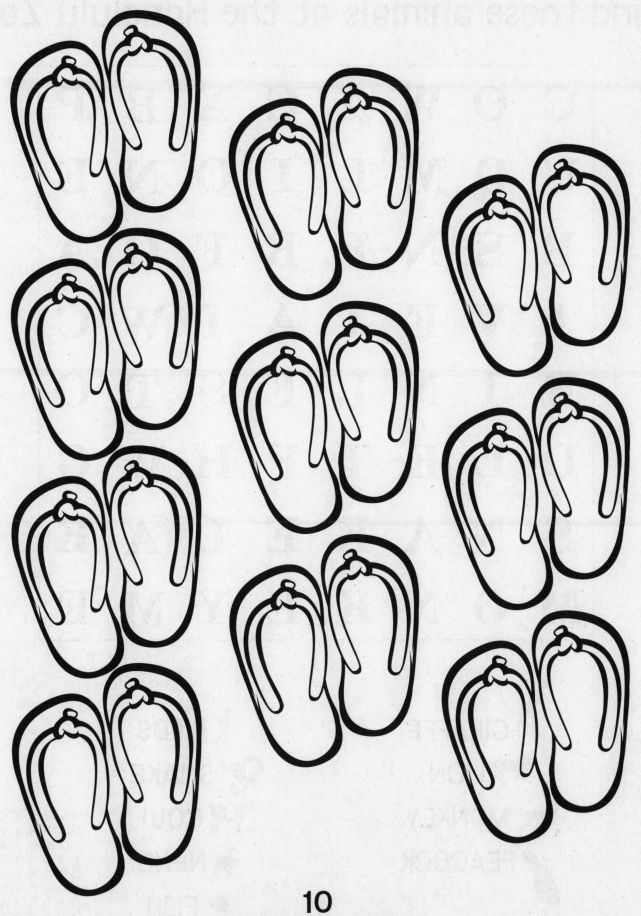

10
Ten Zori (slippers)

Find these animals at the Honolulu Zoo.

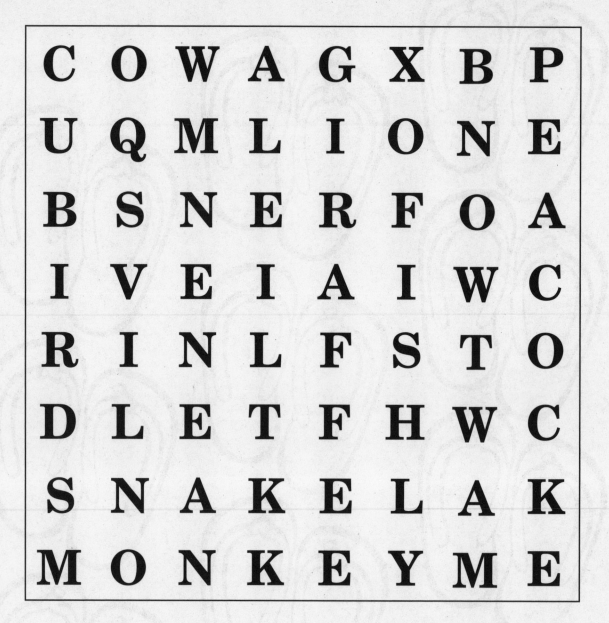

```
C O W A G X B P
U Q M L I O N E
B S N E R F O A
I V E I A I W C
R I N L F S T O
D L E T F H W C
S N A K E L A K
M O N K E Y M E
```

GIRAFFE

LION

MONKEY

PEACOCK

BIRDS

SNAKE

COW

NENE

FISH

Answer

```
M O N K E Y M E
S N A K E L A K
D L E T F H W C
R I N L F S T O
I V E I A I W C
B S N E R F O A
U Q M L I O N E
C O W A G X B P
```

Color by Numbers

1 = Pink   2 = Blue   3 = Gray   4 = Yellow

Help this boy find his slippers.

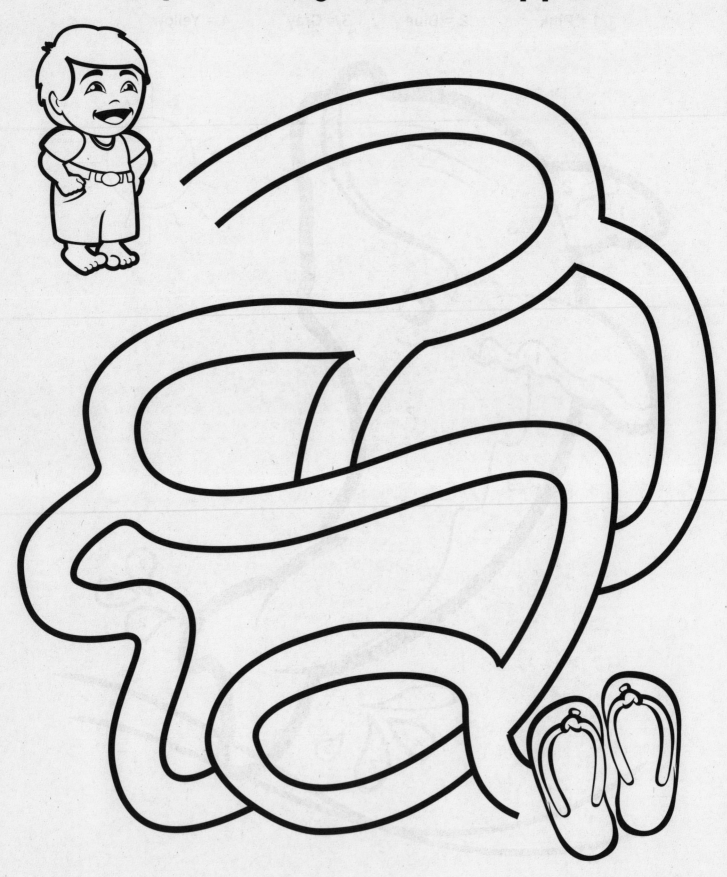